I Want to Be a LION

by Thomas Kingsley Troupe
Illustrated by Melinda Beavers

PICTURE WINDOW BOOKS
a capstone imprint

"Eli, don't you want to see the lions?" my friend Corey asked.

I peeked down into their habitat. A bunch of lions rested in the sunshine.

"They look tired too," I said and yawned. "My baby brother kept everyone awake last night."

"Oh, that's rough," Corey said. "Well, I'm going to check out these big cats."

"Sounds good," I said. "I'll catch up in a minute."

"I want to be a lion," I mumbled as I closed my eyes. "Then I could sleep in peace."

I blinked, and everything changed. I stood on the bench and roared. I WAS a lion! I leaped into the habitat to join the others.

I was hot with all that fur. The sun made me feel even hotter. But finally I could sleep!

"Hey!" a lioness called to me. "You can't nap now! Watch the cubs while I find some food for the pride."

4

Then the zoo habitat was gone. Tall grass waved as far as I could see. With no fences, I could run free forever. The zoo had been nice, but it was nothing like the African savanna.

"Play with us, big guy!" said one of the cubs.

I swatted at the cub and pretended to bite. I also kept watch for danger.

The lionesses attacked the antelope. It was over in seconds. The poor thing didn't have a chance against the hunters.

I felt a fly land on my back. I used my tail to knock it away. It felt weird, like I had an extra arm attached to my rear end!

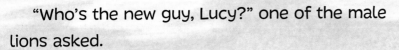

"Who's the new guy, Lucy?" one of the male lions asked.

"This is Eli," she said. "He's new to our pride."

The others nodded at me. The male lions had large, dark manes, but all of the lions had short, light brown fur like mine.

Calling a lion a "big cat" is no joke! Male lions can grow up to 10 feet (3 meters) long and can weigh up to 500 pounds (227 kilograms). Female lions can grow to 9 feet (2.7 m) long and can weigh almost 400 pounds (181 kg).

"Let's eat already," said one of the lions.

"Not so fast," Lucy said. "Here comes Snarl and his pride. They want our food."

The lions coming our way looked mean. Lucy nodded toward them.

"You're up, Eli," Lucy said. "Show them who's king of the savanna."

I ran toward Snarl, and he ran at me. I'd never moved so fast!

Sharp claws popped out of my paws. I swiped at Snarl and knocked him on the head. He scratched back. I opened my mouth to show Snarl my teeth.

Anger rose in my throat, and I let out a HUGE roar! It echoed like there were 10 angry lions out there.

Snarl and his lions left us alone. The lions in my pride seemed happy with me.

"Nice job, Eli!" Lucy said. Her tail swished back and forth. "Time to eat!"

As the lions ate the antelope, I turned away.

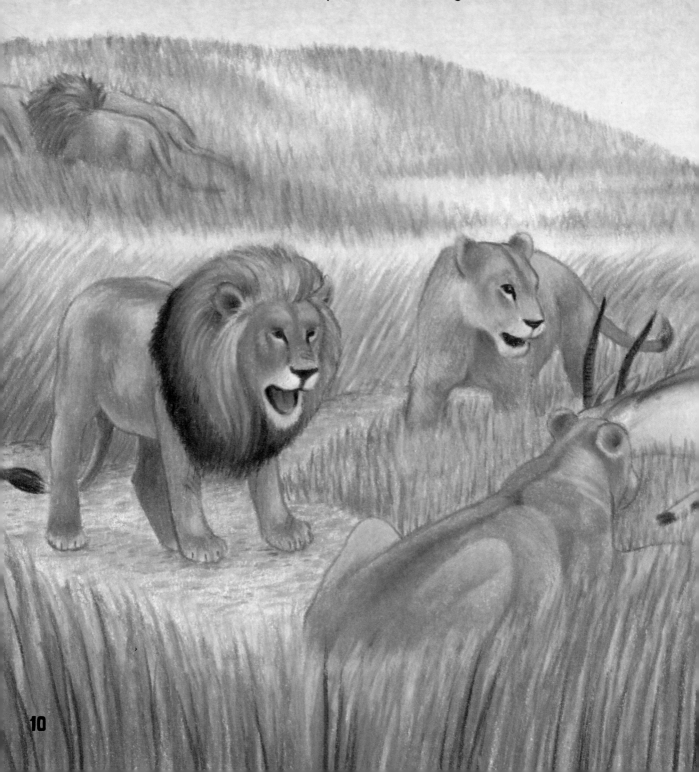

"What's the matter? Not hungry?" another male lion asked.

"Not really," I said.

"I'm sick of antelope," he said.

"Well, what else do you eat?" I asked.

"Oh, all kinds of things," the lion said. "Zebras, wildebeests, giraffes."

"Wow," I said. Suddenly I didn't want to eat ever again.

"If we're really hungry, we might even eat an elephant," he added.

I didn't know lions could attack something so big!

Lions don't always get a big meal. Sometimes they will eat smaller prey such as hares, birds, or reptiles.

I watched a lioness with a big belly walk slowly away from the pride.

"Lilah is off to have her cubs," Lucy said. "She and the cubs won't return for a few months."

I looked around. I wondered where the dad was.

"Does she need someone to protect her?" I asked. "Or help with the cubs?"

"In a group of lionesses, the mothers usually give birth around the same time," Lucy said. "They protect and nurse the cubs together."

A team of lion moms! That's like a furry fighting force of super cats.

"Wow! How many cubs will Lilah have?" I asked.

Lilah's belly looked really huge. There had to be six or seven in there!

"Usually two or three," Lucy said. "They'll stay with Lilah until they're at least 2 years old."

I liked being part of the pride. The other lions wrestled
around. Some of them licked each other's faces.

A little cub rubbed his head against my leg.

"Hi, little guy," I said. He growled like he wanted to play.

"That's Jacques," Lucy said. "Laziest lion I know."

Jacques looked like he was dozing off. I was ready to snooze too.

"We all sleep a lot, but he's the king of naps," Lucy said. "Paws down."

Cat nap? More like a cat deep sleep! Lions can sleep up to 20 hours a day.

"Are those old lions?" I asked with a yawn. They moved a little slower than the rest.

"Yes," Lucy explained. "They're 10 or 11 years old. Most males live until they're about 12. Females usually live a few years longer."

"Whoa," I said, suddenly wide awake. "I'm going to be 12 in a few years!"

Lucy looked at me funny. She didn't know I was human before.

Lions live up to 15 years in the wild and more than 20 years in captivity. Their biggest threats are from humans. People have taken over land where lions once lived. Also, some people hunt lions illegally.

A few trucks drove toward us. Hunters with guns
rode in the back.

"Poachers!" one of the lionesses roared.

I leaped to my paws. Lucy ran toward the trees,
nudging the cubs along. Everyone ran away.

Almost everyone, I realized.

"Jacques!" I roared. I had to wake up that sleepy lion.

He stirred a bit as the trucks rumbled closer.

"Wake up!" someone else yelled.

"Wake up, Eli!" Corey shouted. I jumped up.

"I was just resting my eyes for a second," I said with a yawn.

"We're heading to the next exhibit," Corey said. "C'mon!"

I stood and looked down into the habitat. A lion that resembled Jacques yawned. He looked like he'd just woken up too.

"So much for my cat nap," I said. I waved to my pride before I joined the rest of my class.

The African lion population has dropped by more than half in the last 30 years. Help keep them from becoming extinct. Learn more about lions and support wildlife groups that help these and other amazing animals survive!

Additional facts:

• Male lions defend the pride's territory. That territory may be up to 100 square miles (259 sq. km) of scrub or open grasslands.

• Lion cubs begin hunting when they are 11 months old.

• A lion roars to communicate to members of its pride and to warn other animals (including people!) to stay away.

• When feeding on a large animal, a lion can eat almost 60 pounds (27 kg). It won't need to eat again for several days.

• Lions live in prides of two to 40 cats. The average pride has about 12 cats.

Glossary

extinct—no longer living; an extinct species is one that has died out, with no more of its kind surviving

habitat—the natural place and conditions in which a plant or animal lives

horizon—the line where the sky and the earth or sea seem to meet

nurse—to drink mother's milk

poacher—a person who hunts or fishes illegally

population—a group of people, animals, or plants living in a certain place

prey—an animal hunted by another animal for food

pride—a group or family of lions

reptile—a cold-blooded animal that breathes air and has a backbone; most reptiles lay eggs and have scaly skin

savanna—a flat, grassy area of land with few or no trees

territory—an area of land that an animal claims as its own to live in

Read More

Amstutz, Lisa J. *Lions Are Awesome!* North Mankato, Minn.: Capstone Press, 2015.

Carney, Elizabeth. *Everything Big Cats.* Washington, D.C.: National Geographic Children's Books, 2011.

Throp, Claire. *Lions.* North Mankato, Minn.: Heinemann Raintree, 2014.

FactHound

FactHound offers a safe, fun way to find Internet sites related to this book. All of the sites on FactHound have been researched by our staff.

Here's all you do:
Visit *www.facthound.com*
Type in this code: 9781479568604

Check out projects, games and lots more at
www.capstonekids.com

Index

Books in the Series

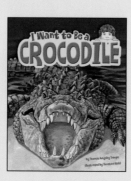

Thanks to our advisers for their expertise, research, and advice:
Micaela Szykman Gunther, PhD
Associate Professor and Chair, Department of Wildlife
Humboldt State University

Editors: Shelly Lyons and Nick Healy
Designer: Sarah Bennett
Creative Director: Nathan Gassman
Production Specialist: Tori Abraham

The illustrations in this book were created using colored pencil with digital editing and effects.
Photograph on pages 20-21: Shutterstock/Volt Collection, page 21: Shutterstock/Adwo

Picture Window Books are published by Capstone,
1710 Roe Crest Drive, North Mankato, Minnesota 56003
www.capstonepub.com

Library of Congress Cataloging-in-Publication Data
Troupe, Thomas Kingsley, author.
 I want to be a lion / by Thomas Kingsley Troupe ; illustrated by Melinda Beavers.
    pages cm. — (Nonfiction picture books. I want to be….)
 Summary: "Text written from the animal's perspective helps teach kids about life as a lion"-- Provided by publisher.
 Audience: Ages 5-8
 Audience: K to grade 3
 Includes bibliographical references and index.
 ISBN 978-1-4795-6860-4 (library binding) —
ISBN 978-1-4795-6864-2 (ebook pdf)
1. Lion—Juvenile literature. I. Beavers, Melinda, illustrator. II. Title.
 QL737.C23T4739 2016
 599.757—dc23
                                    2015010236

Printed in the United States of America in Brainerd, Minnesota.
032015   008826BANGF15